MINI REVERSE
COLORING BOOK

Spark your creativity with this travel-sized reverse coloring book! Transform pre-colored pages into unique artworks by drawing shapes, patterns, and details over vibrant splashes. Let the colors inspire captivating scenes and characters. Experiment with pens, markers, or mixed media to add depth and texture. Compact and portable, it's perfect for stress relief on the go.

HOW TO USE THIS BOOK

1st of all, there are no rules!
Just unleash your imagination and have fun!

Gather Supplies: Reverse coloring book, black pen or marker.
Optional: Colored pens or pencils.

Find a Page: Pick a colorful page you like.

Look Closely: Notice the shapes and colors.

Start Drawing: Use your pen to outline shapes and add details.

Add More Details: Draw patterns, doodles and add extra touches.

Have Fun: Enjoy the creative process and relax!

(The pages for testing your pens are located in the back of the book)

BEFORE
Waiting for your creativity

AFTER

Unleash your creativity

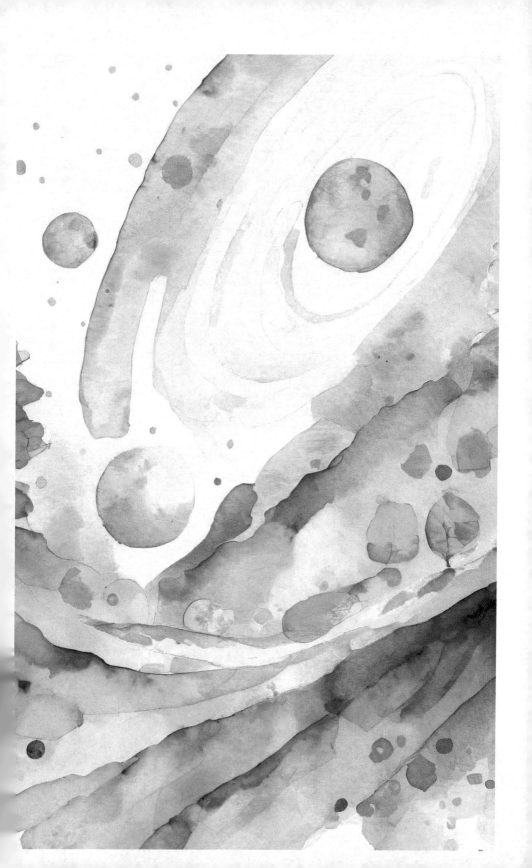

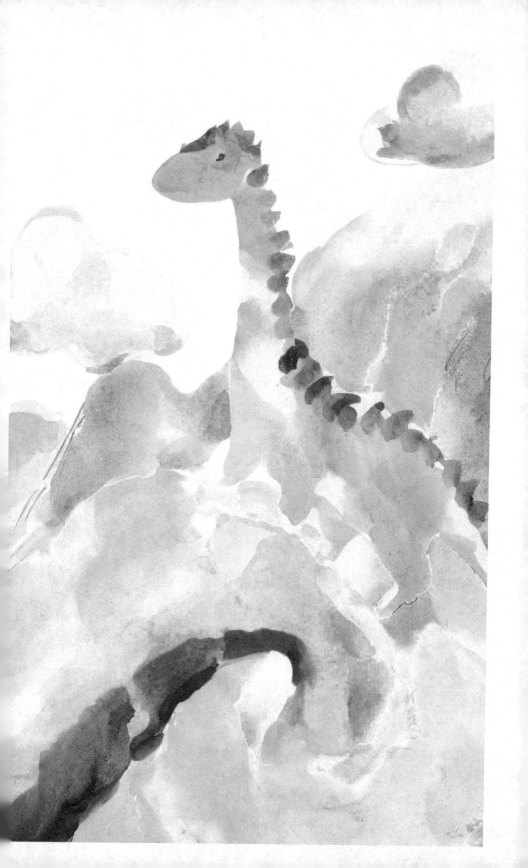

PEN TEST PAGE

Use this page to test the color and thickness of your pens

PEN TEST PAGE

Use this page to test the color and thickness of your pens

Made in the USA
Las Vegas, NV
18 December 2024

14956328R00056